Chocolate City: Love For A Woman

Lewis Stewart III

Chocolate City: Love For A Woman
Copyright © 2024 by Lewis Stewart III.

All rights reserved. No part of this publication may be reproduced, distributed, or transmitted in any form or by any means, including photocopying, recording, or other electronic or mechanical methods, without the written consent of the publisher. The only exceptions are for brief quotations included in critical reviews and other non-commercial uses permitted by copyright law.

MILTON & HUGO L.L.C.
4407 Park Ave., Suite 5
Union City, NJ 07087, USA

Website: *www.miltonandhugo.com*
Hotline: *1- 888-778-0033*
Email: *info@miltonandhugo.com*

Ordering Information:
Quantity sales. Special discounts are granted to corporations, associations, and other organizations. For more information on these discounts, please reach out to the publisher using the contact information provided above.

Library of Congress Control Number:	2024912436
ISBN-13: 979-8-89285-196-1	[Paperback Edition]
979-8-89285-195-4	[Digital Edition]

Rev. date: 06/10/2024

To the women who influenced my life, I salute you while you are here and the afterlife.

Dedicated to my wife Paulette who was my inspiration in writing these poems.

Contents

A Daughter	1
Beautiful	3
Beauty in the Beholder	4
Behind Every Man	5
Being a Woman	7
Black is Beautiful	8
Black Woman	9
Brown Sugar	11
Cherish Love	13
Chocolate Lighting	15
Dark Skinned Woman	16
Dear Black Woman	17
Dear Wife	18
Describing a Mother	19
Face of a Black Woman	21
Falling In Love with You	22
For You My Wife	23
Hot Cocoa	24
Hot Sauce	25
How Much I Love You	27
I Have Love for You	28
Light skinned woman	30
Love Always	31
Making Love	33
Most Beautiful Woman in the World	35
My Lady Forever	36
My Pleasure	38
Oriental Petal	39
Power of Love	41
Pretty Woman	42
Self-Worth	43
Sisterhood	44
Sisters	46
Strong Woman	48

Super Woman..49
Sweet Thing...51
Tan Salsa 52
Thinking About You..54
Vanilla Cream 55
Wedding Cheer..57
What A Man Sees in a Woman 58
What I Look For In A Woman... 60
What Is A Good Woman 62
Why I am Light-Skinned.. 64
You Are The Reason..65

A Daughter

A daughter is a girl or woman who was made by her parents.
Who is created by God.
A daughter has meaning.
A stepdaughter, an adopted daughter, or a daughter-in-law.

A daughter carries the characteristics of her mother.
She is protected by her father.
She will fight for her father's attention.
As her mother role teaching her how to be a lady.

She is like a star shining with joy and happiness.
Starting off as a baby, a teen, a young woman, and an adult.
She brings tears to the parents.
As she enters the world.

A daughter needs her father's love.
To learn as she gets older the meaning of love.
She illuminates the night sky.
Igniting fireworks of all different colors.

She has been treated so gently.
Her face glows over an entire room.
She is an angel.
Passing the sweetness to her unborn children.

She is the cuteness of her parents.
She listens to her parents.
As she starts to become within her own.
Telling her she can become anything she wants.

Finally finding that someone.
Whose name she will inherit.
Receiving the blessing of her father
As she prepares to leave the nest.

She ventures out into the world to spread her inner self.
Getting all the nourishments to conquer the world.
Taking on a task that all women must endure.
I am strong. I am ready.

Beautiful

When I was in town, I did not know other serving what I was there for.
I was over a friend's house hanging out.
I was leaving and saw my friend as he just moved there.
As we were talking, I said I have that picture.
He told his wife to get that picture as she did.
My heart was like if she real light skinned will I give it a chance which was not my flavor.
Once she returned with the pictures because you were/are black and beautiful, so I said damn.
They looked at me as I said to them you are very pretty.
That phone call that night I was nervous and scared because I did not know what it would become.
I was happy I had a beautiful woman and should put in more work in keeping my women happy.
I got lazy which was a mistake. I promised will not make that mistake again!!!
A man who has a beautiful wife is a jealous man.
I pray that your soul recommits to me.
Your 😊 smile won me over.
Your ♥ is what I fell in love with.
This make sound corny, but this is my feelings.

Beauty in the Beholder

I love dark skinned woman.
With all my heart.
They are the greatest species on earth.
They are the strongest of all mankind.

I love the way they are built.
The attitude that can motivate a man.
The eye in the sky.
The shadow on the ground.

Her lips that make a man go wild.
The touch of her hands makes a man tingle.
The sheer lotion body.
Make the oil in the skin brightens.

I love the way she moves.
I love the way she sits.
The statue like know other.
Make a man cross the burning sands.

She has that beauty.
That can stop a train in its tracks.
I love the dark skin woman.
Confidence she does not lack.

Behind Every Man

Behind every successful man.
There is a real woman behind the scenes.
She does not want the spotlight but respect.
As the man faces the positive and negative of society or the workforce.

She tells him the truth.
She gives him hope.
She feeds him the nourishment to keep striving for success.
She bears his children.

She takes care of the children.
She takes care of the household.
She becomes the head of the house.
As the man battles to keep the lifestyle intact.

She is his voice in making decisions.
She has an extra ear and mouthpiece.
She does not say anything publicly.
As she stands behind her man as he stands in the hotbox.

He worries about the pressures outside the household.
As she protects the home and family.
As she is his confidant, his sounding board.
She gives him more guidance as she is neutral from the power makers.

No one ever talks about her.
As she stays out of the limelight.
She wants to voice her man in silence.
As he asks her what direction he should travel.

Behind every man is a woman.
Many times, you do not see her at all.
Is it by design or protocol.
Whether it is deliberate or on purpose.
She is not following a script.
She is taking a role that many will not understand.
Behind every man is a woman.

Being a Woman

As I wake up today from last night.
My soul is to believe that I am strong.
To uphold the everyday struggles.
To end the day and night happy.

I am a woman without boundaries.
I am a woman without limits.
I am a woman without constraints.
I am a woman without assumptions.

I feed off positive words of encouragement.
I feed off positive words of wisdom.
I feed off positive words of love.
I feed off positive words of enlightenment.

I fight off all the challenges.
Whether it is simple or difficult.
I am in a world that is dominated by men.
I too must make my place in history.

I am a mother.
I am a daughter.
I am a sister.
I am a niece.
I am a grandmother.
I am an aunt.
I am a cousin.
I am a wife.
I am a friend.

Black is Beautiful

My complexion of my skin tone is diversity.
The uniqueness of my race is evolution.
The courage I display within.
I will let it roar like a lion.

What I see in the mirror.
I am beautiful figure made by GOD.
Black is a prestigious color.
It represents all the elements of mankind.

Black had kings and queens.
Black has always been the peak of the mountain.
From the beginning of time to the present.
It can't be taken or substituted.

The color signifies honor and character.
No one can change my mind.
Look at me, all of my black features.
A stunning growth of beauty.
That can't be denied.

Black is Beautiful.
All day.
Every day.

Black Woman

Black Queen sits high above her throne.
No one another race can replace you.
Your heart is full of gold.
Fill with your strong genes.
Your nurture that keeps the family together.
Your stylist ways shine like the sun.
The glow of your smile is as bright as the moon.

Black Woman

Your spirit is the sound of the hymn of the church.
Loving to the birth of her children.
Your ebony is free and strong.
Black does not crack.
The skin becomes preserve.
As the oils inside the body starts to ooze.
Protecting the likeness that on a black woman can hold.

Black Woman

The world can be cruel.
She fights through the struggles every day.
She seen as weak.
Society is afraid.
She has the power to change the atmosphere.
As a walk of confidence.
Her desires shall not be denied.

Black Woman

Your gentle hands.
Can inspire an army of black men.
The centerpiece of the family.

That build walls to protect her village.
She will sacrifice herself.
For the good of the family.
Nothing like a black woman which has compassion.

Black Woman

She can be heard.
Silent as the night.
She will roar out of anger.
If confronted by a threat.
She holds the world on her chest.
Navigating the tornadoes that seeks to destroy the living.
Black Woman

From a little girl to a grown woman.
From a servant to a leader.
From a princess to a queen.
Rising from oppression.
Growing.
Trusting.
Giving.
Caretaking.
Reliance.
Strength.
Power.
Precious.
Loving.
Emotional.
Independence.

I am a Black Woman.
I am a Black Woman.
I am not a Wonder Woman.
I am a Black Woman.

Brown Sugar

I am going to tell you about this girl.
Who was sent into my world.
Her eyes are like the bright lights on a car.
Her body is smooth like a chocolate candy bar.

The way we kiss is like no other way.
Got me going crazy that's how I behave.
That's that kissing that I have been missing.
How she performs I am not going to mention.

Brown Sugar, getting high with your love.
Got to have that Brown Sugar.

She's delicious like Black Eyed Peas.
Her figure brings me down to my knees.
Got me say ooh baby please.
She can be serious, but she can be a teaser.

Skin is caramel with cocoa eyes.
Groom to the tee.
Smell so sweet.
Make me go wild, that's what you do to me.

Brown Sugar, getting high with your love.
Got to have that Brown Sugar.

This is how the story goes.
Strong genes with the sexy nose.
Standing in a position with her body froze.
She's more than a flower, she is a bright red rose.

She has the wit to get me sprung.
Blinking one eye and linking her tongue.
You don't hear me.
Making love to her is sweet.

Brown Sugar, getting high with your love.
Got to have that Brown Sugar.

I want some of that Brown Sugar.
I want some of that Brown Sugar.
Oh yes, I do.

Cherish Love

I love you with all my heart.
I promise to make you happy.
Everyday with you will be a holiday.
Enjoying being in each other company.

My life without you will not be the same.
Like a caterpillar turns into a butterfly with limited life span.
Even when we argue, my love for you does not diminish.
Even if I did not start it I still love you.

Disagreements do not last.
Our love for each other will.
I am you lover.
You are my lover.

I never met anyone like you.
You touched my heart like anyone never has before.
My mind is on you all the time.
My eyes widen as we sit across the candlelight.

I love you with every breathe I take.
The gleam in your eyes make me stay awake.
When I feel I am losing sight.
A picture of you makes my smile bright.

We shall walk alone together.
We shall dance together.
We shall eat together.
We shall pray together.
We shall celebrate life together.
We shall mourn together.
We shall sit together.
We shall share things together.

We shall lift each other up.
We shall be committed to each other.

Chocolate Lighting

When it is lightning in the sky.
It lights up the earth as it looks to strike.
Walking with purpose.
Compelled to the stare, at sights of the unknown.

Causing attention and beneath all the makeup.
Hiding there underneath, streaking across the floor
Heels touching the ground as thunder roaring across the sky.
Men screaming, we want more.

The moment that come and went.
A brisk of time pass.
Flashes of light, lights up the earth.
Wondering who will be blinded by her beauty.

All stay quiet as they know the batteries are still charge.
When it come and gone, you will remember.
A flash in a moment's notice.
All hail that chocolate lightning.

At an instance can take your heart.
At a blink of an eye can steal your soul.
Who can a person run to.
Who can protect from the lightning.

She is all powerful.
She is mysterious.
She is a woman.
She is a queen.
She is YOU. I am ME.

A QUEEN to be.

Dark Skinned Woman

The image of a dark skin woman is fascinating.
It defines her image and her natural skin tone.
The way she walks, talks, facial expressions, sits, and thinks.
She does not need the sound of music to announce her presence.
Her movement speaks for herself.
She does not have to dance to get attention.
The energy throughout her body is enough to have others drawn to others.
She wants that strong black man to be by her side.
She has the strength to be the matriarch of the entire family.
She is not a colored woman; she is a dark-skinned woman.
All a proud woman.
Oozing with confidence.
As many rivers connect to the Mississippi River.
All woman is connected to the dark-skinned woman.

Dear Black Woman

You were created by GOD.
Through your mother and father.
You grew up to be a beautiful lady.
You are beautiful just the way you are.

You are thoughtful.
You are creative.
You are kind.
You are intelligent.

You are beautiful.
You are natural.
You are gorgeous.
Your skin is divine.

You are a superstar.
You are elite.
You are on of a kind.
You are the rock of the family.

You are a queen.
Show your talents to the world.
Never bashed yourself.
Show the world that you are worthy.

Dear Wife

We are thee if two become one.
If a man loves his wife as a wife loves, her husband.
I have pride in my love for you.
All the riches can't pay me to leave you.
No million woman can pull me away from you.
I have the prize that can't be brought.
When I see your face.
No other woman can take your place.
When I was gone in a warzone.
I thought of you before and after the mission.
I couldn't think of you in the middle had to stay focus.
If I was not careful, I couldn't make it back home to you.
You always stayed committed.
Raising two kids while I was gone but you did it.
You are going through emotions so I understand.
You are appreciated by me.

Describing a Mother

How to describe a mother?
She is the queen of the family.
A mother is Godly.
A mother is nourishing.
A mother is loving.
A mother is compassionate.
A mother is safe.
A mother is caring.
A mother is protective.
A mother is strong.
A mother is kind.
A mother is tough.
A mother is unique.
A mother is a caretaker.
A mother is a sponge.
A mother is peaceful.
A mother is a fire starter.
A mother is magnificent.
A mother is humble.
A mother is knowledgeable.
A mother is wonderful.
A mother is tough.
A mother is awesome.
A mother is pure.
A mother is honest.
A mother is tender.
A mother is bold.
A mother is wise.
A mother is powerful.
A mother is endearment.
A mother is attractive.
A mother is a bad mama jama.
A mother is warm.

A mother is a teacher.
A mother is a provider.
A mother is a leader amongst her child or children.
A mother is the second in command of the grandmother.
A mother is the extension of her nephews and nieces.
A mother is influencer.
A mother is a sounding board.
A mother tells the facts of life.
A mother can be stern in the right moments.
A mother has a gift of talking.
A mother is an educator.
A mother is a survivor.
What is your mother?

Face of a Black Woman

My hair is made of wavy wool.
My nose is genetically unique.
My figure is shape like a coke bottle.
My eyes sparkles like the stars in the sky.

Compared to another race of women.
A face of a black woman stands out.
Powerful but sensitive.
My ears are like a shell sounding of ocean waves.

My face can signal many things.
Discipline my kids respected by my king.
Face of a black women gets older.
It does not crack just gets finer.

The oils inside my body.
Keeps the skin moisture.
Protects it from harm rays from the sun.
Preserve in the time of death.

Only one kind of a black face.
Other races may be different but share to same color.
Black face stands out.
Always will be remembered.

Falling In Love with You

I think I am in love with you.
You make me feel like a new person.
At first, I liked you but nothing special.
Now I am feeling you so much.

When I had a bad day, you cheered me up.
When I got dirty you cleaned me up.
I melt when we hug tightly.
Your energy makes me excited.

I love when we cuddle under a blanket.
Watching the sunrise on the porch.
During my days I can't stop thinking about you.
I have daydreams about you.

It is hard sometimes to concentrate,
We started out as strangers.
We make our way to friends.
We quickly became lovers.

I waited for you for so long.
I took my time as I was hurt before.
I can not resist the felling I have for you.
Sometimes in life you get that one chance.

I went ahead to make the move.
I did not want to lose my place in securing you.
I felt you should belong to me.
As I was falling in love with you.

For You My Wife

Loving you my wife has no end.
Loving you is everything.
From everything for the beginning.

No magnitude of earthquakes.
Beyond my comprehension.
Your love will bring me home.

You lit a passionate fire in me.
Which I had hidden for a long time.
You are bringing out the me that was locked in a box.

I wanted to expose my creative side.
But hide it away from so long.
Sorry I did not share it with you.

Sometimes it is better late than never.
I hope it is not too late.
Many words I want to share with you.

If I could rip off my skin and show my flesh.
You can see all the emotions in my body.
Sorry I did not share my pain all the time.

I had to keep the wall as my protection.
Afraid that I would be hurt.
I did not mean anything bad things between us.

I should have let you in more.
I promised I will not withhold my thoughts ever again.
I want my wife, lover, and best friend.

Hot Cocoa

When you walk in a room it is so smooth.
Your smile puts others into a groove.
Your lips are as sweet as syrup.
Your skin is smooth as a baby bottom.

The aroma of your perfume is stunning.
It brings out the feeling and the emotions.
Picture on the front of the magazine titled Essence
Pours in a cup of steamy enjoyment.

Waiting for the moment to be tasted.
Flowing freely throughout the body.
Who is this woman this man desires?
Who is this woman this man can't deny?

Who is this woman that has this brown cloth?
To wipe her mouth before licking the taste from her lips.
The waiting moments of enjoyment.
The satisfaction of the mood that burst within.

This is a great time to be hot.
I am glad you are cocoa.
The best color in the world.
Taught that since you were a little girl.

Hot Sauce

Our hair can be described as fine silky or an Afro.
Our eyes can be hazel, brown, blue or green.
Our skin can be dark brown or light.
Our mixture can be of shapes and tones.

Our personality is friendly and cheerful.
We talked with my hands.
When we are talking, we put my emotions.
With intensity and passion of our expressions.

We greet everyone with a good morning.
Even if we are strangers passing by.
Our culture is all about family.
We are hard-working and strong.

We will fight for my rights and others during adversity.
We are loyal to my lover ones until death part us.
We embrace diversity in the world.
We have an eye for fashion.

We are independent women.
We know how to work through obstacles.
We come in a variety of sizes and shapes.
We carry a petite figure with a coke bottle shape.

We dress both conservatively and traditionally that goes back in our history.
We are hospitable and have deep spiritual beliefs.
We fight for what is right.
Standing in the face of inequality and unfairness.

Sometimes we can be head strong even if we are wrong.
Later think about it and talk about it so get the proper understanding.
We are a welcoming race of females.
That make beautiful babies with any mix.

Some mistake us as loud and aggressive.
We are just expressing ourselves to the world.
We are very friendly and generous.
We are educated professionals.

How Much I Love You

You are in my heart.
Where you are supposed to be.
That door is locked.
You the only one that has the key.

You are the mother of my children.
You are the one who keeps me going.
You are my friend, my lover, my soul, and my wife.

I never fought for anyone before.
I let them go as needed.
You are special to me.
I am not trying to let you go.

I do not want to argue with you.
Just want to have a peaceful conversation.
Yes, we can disagree.
We should also respect each other feelings.

I love you more than any woman before you.
I will not love another woman while I am with you.
You belong to me and me only.
Your heart beats for me and my heart beats no doubt beat for you.

I love you. I love you.
Actions speaks louder than words.
My actions are in a class by itself.
I will go through fire to get to you.
I will take a bullet for you.

I love you like that.

I Have Love for You

I am not a toy.
I am not your friend.
I am something that you never can pretend.
I have been faithful to you.
I never lie.
I am here until you die.

I'll never leave you.
You my only man.
I have something that you will never understand.
No need to worry.
No need to cry.
I have doubts and you know the reasons why.

I Have Love For You.
Baby, I will give it if you want me too.

You are a bad boy.
I am a rose on a bud.
You had a flavor.
That made me fall in love.
Your children I conceived.
I was something that you wanted to believe.

The feeling I had was concealed.
Plenty of times I had to forgive.
Life is too short, but I want to be with you.
Spent half my life connecting to my boo.
Sometimes you make me happy.
Sometimes you make me sad.
Special gift I have is my babies dad.

I Have Love For You.
Baby, I will give it to you if you want me too.

I will give you one more time.
My heart is mines.
Can't disappoint it on a drop of a dime.
Can't cause me worry.
Can't make me cry.
Next time it could be a good-bye.

It's just electricity in human nature.
Which electrons are trying to feed.
If you can handle that I know you can believe.
I am a dove.
Flying to find love.
If you are not the one to give love.
Darling if you want me.
You must prove your worth.
As I think to fly away.
But I can't leave.
Because my love for you is still there.

I Have Love For You.
Baby, I will give it to you if you want me too.

I Have Love For You.
Baby, I will give it to you if you want me too.

Light skinned woman

I like how your hair catches the light.
It looks like the sunlight feeds your hair all the vitamins.
It is so healthy and matches your glow.

Your body is so smooth.
You can be described as a red bone or light bread.
Nicknames we give to beautiful woman that builds self-confidence.

How does your beautiful face brighten up the day?
Everyone sees how you smile and brings joy to others.
I love you like the clouds in the sky.

I love your shaped figure.
Your body shakes and jiggles like jello.
You have all the flavors that is a delight.

Your eyes stand out with the rest of your body.
Your energy out matches the sun.
Your coolness is brighter than a full moon.

You are positive and uplifting.
You are radiant with your movement.
Look at me. I am so stunning.

Love Always

Baby what you are to me.
I wanted to you to make a family.
We always give us joy.
Stay together always.

Love is very precious.
Like the clouds up above.
I think of no one else.
You all that I love.

I know life can be hard.
I know life can be true.
I know I love you.
I know you love me.

Give a brother a chance to see his change.
My heart is torn.
I shed tears night after night.
Wishing I had you in my arms.

I miss your demeanor.
I miss your smile.
I miss you communication.
I miss your style.

You are lovely.
You are beautiful.
You are so fine.
Like an expensive glass of wine.

I need you back.
I need you to feel for me again.
I need my girl back.
I need to support her to the end.

God Bless us during this rough times.
God will see us through.
God loves the both of us.
God will bring us back together.
In Jesus name, I say AMEN.

Making Love

Love heightens our emotions and awakens our senses.
Sweet like the aroma of flowers.
Drowning in the wetness that our bodies created.
Our eyes locked in heavy passion.
We are intact all night long.

I want to make love to you.

The sounds are like music.
The mist rising in the air.
The thrusting sounds that the room makes.
Like roses no other flower can compare.
As the bodies heat up, the sweet smell of the sense in the air.

I want to make love to you.

A candle that has a burning flame.
When you wiggle your body.
As we keep going to the break of dawn.
The lights are off and we start to morn.
Giving some good loving.

I want to make love to you.

I feel good lying next to you.
I am so strung. I am so strung.
Making love to you.
As I paralyze in the bed.
As you get your towel.

I want to make love to you.

I need it. I need it. I need it.
Like an addicted drug.

I want your touch.
It's driving me crazy.
Come on. Come on. Come on.

I want to make love to you.

Both of us rolling ion the sheets.
Until our loving making is complete.
When we do, it's just you and me.
When your legs are part.
And releasing the juices from me.

I want to make love to you.

Let's make some sweet love.
Let's get busy.
Afterwards hod each other all night long.
Let's do it again and again.
Like young rabbits for the first time.

I want to make love to you.
I want to make love to you.
My body is out of control.
My body calms me down.
You are the only controllable force.
Can hold me down?

I want to make love to you.
I want to make love to you.
I want to make love to you.
I want to make love to you.
I want to make love to you.

My lady.
My lady.
My lady.

Most Beautiful Woman in the World

From a man to a loving woman.
You are the winner of the World's Universe.
One of the greatest honors in the world.

You are the most beautiful woman in the world.
Heaven cast a mold with your beauty.
The prettiest woman not a fairy tale.

Your smile eases my pain.
Your face can heel many sorrows.
The Lord design you with tender loving care.

Your friendship in the beginning I held.
More precious than silver, gold, and diamonds.
If you ever knew what power, you hold in your hands.

What a nice voice you have that carries.
You are an angel that was sent from above.
Those cheeks attached to the joy on your face.

Let me count the clouds.
How many you will find.
Your presence reaches from end to end.

My life changed the moment I met you.
Beauty is all but rare.
You are so beautiful, if not the world but I will care.

My Lady Forever

So, you have agreed to marry me.
It makes me so happily.
Life is more than precious.
Now we can raise a family.
There was never a doubt in our minds.
You can count on me.
I'll never let you down.
Lady, you always believe in me.

You and I are like glue.
We get pulled apart by the magic.
Brings us back to together.
Our Holy Spirits will not let us break away.
We fell in love and our babies were born.
Growing up on how we wanted them to be.
Both of us keeping them warm.

My Lady Forever.
I'm holding you close.
It's like a dream.
I can't picture an empty scene.
We are a team.
If I ever lose you.
Where will I go.
Life would have no meaning.

Sometimes we must go through hell.
To get where we want to be.
God takes us through it.
So, we can be stronger than ever.
He keeps us grounded.
He keeps the devil away.
Keeping us steady by praying every day.

We can start over.
To make this last.
No other one will have our backs.
But the both of us.
As the river flows downwards.
Rain falling from the sky.
Our dreams can become reality.

We say what we mean.
Continue to work it out.
We can be proof in the pudding.
Without a window to throw it out.
You my lady forever.
I want to be your man forever.
Both of us are together forever.

Forces are out there.
To destroy human lives.
Dressing in a costume in human disguise.
We must identify the fraud.
To live in peace.
Growing old together.
Until eternality.

And I say we made it from the start.
We made it day after day.
We made it night after night.
We fell so far in love.
We are in love.
No force should split us up.
No force should tear us up.
No force should ever come between us.

My Pleasure

It is my pleasure to have a wife like you.
I felt that you love me for me.
You did not have to flake.
You were not fake.
A city girl who fell in love with a country boy.

I never thought I would get a city girl like you.
I thought I was the man when I got you.
You wanted to have a life with me.
You had my children.
You love me from pole to pole.

I want that love back.
As I am not the guy I once was.
I had to be humble.
As you choose to be with me.
It's my pleasure that you are with me.

I am holding on to my true love.
No one loves me as you do.
Our heart happy in that I will sacrifice.
Your heart belongs to me.
I love you with all my heart.

My love. My love. My love.
Oh, my love. I love you to the end of days.
My love forever.

Oriental Petal

I am a dedicate, polite, and shy petal.
I come from a culture that is strict in values.
I am seen as the opposite of what the world views.
I come from a culture that is open-minded and wide open.

I like it when I get complimented.
I like it when I get something that my beauty is focused on.
My demeanor is very reserved.
Many mistake it as being timid.

I am very intelligent.
My love is expressed with actions not just words.
I want to maintain harmony among others.
Avoiding conflicts with the opposite of sex of my culture.

I want a male who is confident and independent.
I love a man with a great sense of humor.
I prefer a man who have dreams and ambitions.
The attractive traits such as honesty and sincerity.

I appreciate a gentle.
Not a man to treat me below his equal.
I am charming, petite, and soft.
A few qualities that all men can handle.

My skin is silky, smooth, and hairless.
I believe in marriage for life.
I will stick with him through the best and worst of times.
My eyes can be shaped as round, narrow, or deep-set.

I value tradition.
I value maturity.
I do not keep a grudge.
As the body is my temple to cleanse.
I am Asian.

Power of Love

Out of the sky that shadows me.
Whether North and South
Or East and West.
I thank GOD.
In brings you to my soul.

You not by my side.
I cry alone.
Under my deep breath.
You will not be alone.
As you are my power source.

Love does strange things.
To an Alpha man.
Her sense of awareness.
Her nature by intuitions.
That brings us closer together.

The letters I write.
Means more the words I type.
Still the same meaning.
One is a little riper.
Day and night.
The power of love is still there.

Pretty Woman

Pretty woman where beauty lies.
Sparkle in your eyes represents a zillion stars.
The strive of your steps.
The width of your hips.
The curl of your full lips.

A phenomenal of a woman.
Just as cool as the fall air.
Attractive as bees are lured to honey.
The flash of bright white teeth.
As you walk, men fall in their minds.

But they can't touch.
Maybe it is a mystery.
How you arch your back.
The rise of your breasts.
That is the essence of you.

The swing of my waist.
The happiness of my feet.
My head is held up.
I talk with poise.
Means the grace of my style.

Now you understand.
I don't shout.
The ethnicity of my hair.
When you see me in passing.
Should make you proud.

The palm of my hands.
In need of my care.
I am a phenomenal of a woman.
My present you better beware.

Self-Worth

Look at me.
No one can judge me.
I am a human being.
I deserve to be respected.
When it is all said at the end.
I am entitled to share my thoughts.
I am educated.
I am smart.
I bring a lot to a relationship.
I bring a lot to society.
I bring a lot to the workplace.
I am a dime of dozen.
My self-esteem is high.
High as the night skies.
I do not have to compare myself to others.
I shall not underestimate my self-worth.

Sisterhood

Sisterhood is a band of women that form a relationship outside of being relative.
It takes the place of not having a blood sister or replace a loss of a sister.
It emphasizes a relationship between women.
They demonstrate the power women must impact society.

The relationship that can last forever.
A special relationship that is built on trust.
A special relationship that is built on love.
A special relationship that is built on understanding.
A special relationship that is built on respect.
A special relationship that is built on feelings.

Sisters in sisterhood share emotions.
The ability to laugh together.
The ability to cry together.
The ability to share a moment together.
The ability to share joy.
The ability to share sorrow.
To pull each other through the rough times.

The connection is a deep hole that is endless.
The strength is powerful.
They uplift each other.
They challenge each other.
They are honest with each other.
They care for one another.
They embrace their family as their own.

Sisterhood is described in so many ways.
It is called a union.
It is called an alliance.
It is called a community.
It is called a fellowship.
It is called a village.

Sisterhood means keeping each other secrets.
Sisterhood means be each other confidantes.
Sisterhood means encourage each other.
Sisterhood means support each other.
Sisterhood means belonging to a group as close-knit family.

Sisters

What is a sister?
A woman or girl related to another female of the same parents.
Or another female related to the mother or father.
Or female that was adopted into the family.
Or a female mother or father married another person with a daughter.

She is your cheerleader.
She is your harshest critic.
She makes you think.

She knows your strengths.
She knows your weakness.
She knows your tolerance.

She is in your corner.
She tells you what you do not want to hear.
She could be older or younger in the siblings' line up.

She will stand up for you.
She will be truthful with you.
She acknowledges you when you are wrong.

A sister is loyal to you.
A sister is protective of you.
She has been there every milestone with you.

A sister accepts you for who you are.
A sister respects each other secrets.
A sister knows how to make you feel.

A sister family is your family.
Sisters have that special relationship.
Sisters are the extensions of their mother or mothers.

Sisters are each other sounding boards.
Sisters are each other soulmates.
Twin, triplets, or more are thinks as one.

Sisters are mindful of each other space.
Sisters are supportive of each other.
Sisters can communicate for hours.

Strong Woman

I am a strong woman.
From head to toe.
I am bold.
I am intelligent.
I am sweet.
I am fire.
I am desirable.
I am a firecracker if need be.
I am cool.
I can cook.
I can take care of my family.
I can give others sound advice.
I can be low key.
I can communicate very well.
I can bring home the bacon.
I enjoy dancing.
I enjoy signing.
I love having a good time.
I like to be along sometimes.
I am a good woman.
I am a good wife.
I am a good mother.
I am a good daughter.
I am a good sister.
I am a good aunt.
I am a good cousin.
I am a good grandmother.
I am a good friend.

Super Woman

Woman wants to know where I get my superpowers from.
When I want into a room just cool as a fan.
I can take care of my kids and my man.
I glue that keeps our family tight nit.

I am a Super Woman.

I endure the struggles as a female every day.
Always proving I am the right fit.
My ideas get passed on but ultimately use for solutions.
As I must prove myself day after day.

I am a Super Woman.

Men themselves think they know better.
I listen as I fill in their blanks.
I sing when I hear music.
I dance when I like a song.

I am a Super Woman.

The burning fire in my eyes.
Will not let me fail.
My head will not bow.
I make heads turn as I twist my hips.

I am a Super Woman.

When moments get too much.
I take an inhale deep breath.
Along with the rise of my breasts.
I slowly exhale back down to normal.

I am a Super Woman.

There is nothing I can't handle.
When you pass by me.
Know you are in the presence of a real woman.
Part of the brave and the bold.
I was born ready for the world.

I am a Super Woman.
That's who I am.

Sweet Thing

I love your beautiful skin tone.
The smoothness of your body.
The slick smell of your hair.
Your breath smelling like sweet chocolate.

You have fire in your heart.
Like lightning in the sky.
You mind is like gold.
Precious is what is to behold.

You can't be denied.
Your strength and courage are stealth.
The compassion of your soul.
As the heat rises, the snow brings cold.

You are so dedicated.
Sweet as honey.
Melt like sugar.
Fine as wine.

Your eyes fit every description.
Carmel
Hassle
Almond
And all the rest.

It's just like candy.
Smell like cake.
Softy as ice cream.
Rich like caramel.

Sweet Thing.
Sweet Thing.

Tan Salsa

A Hispanic woman is dedicated.
She is loyal.
Her wears her emotions on her heart and soul.
She is the matriarch of her family.

She is family oriented.
She is passionate.
She has supportive woman around her.
She is emotional and fiery.

She has a strong sense of culture.
She has a strong sense of tradition.
She loves to be loved.
She gives too much of herself.

Her statue is a large front.
Her thick toned thighs.
Her circular round hips.
Her large eyes that can hypnotize you.

Her warm skin tone hakes the colors
Chestnut
Amber
Orange
Gold

With shades of color
Blue
Burgundy
Teal
Purple.

She values religion, family, food, and music.
She believes in celebrations.
She loves salsa dancing.
She loves and inspires other to have fun.

She is brave.
She put herself in harm's way.
She stands by her man.
She is a loving woman.

Thinking About You

I think about you every day.
I think about you when I eat.
I think about you when I sleep.
I think about you when I am awake.
I think of you when I drive.

I think about you when I walk.
I think about you when I talk.
I think about you when I am chill'n.
I think about you when I am day dreaming.
I think about you when I work out.

I think about you when I am out.
I think about you when I write.
I think about you when I type.
I think thing about you when I clean.
I think thing about you when I work.

I think about you daily.
I think about you.
When you are in love with a person.
It comes naturally.
Because I am thinking about you.

Vanilla Cream

My skin is very plain and exciting.
I have unique and interesting qualities.
I am notable in a memorable type of way.
My smoothness is sweet and creamy.

Comforting sensation is the sweet smell of desert.
Can trigger happy memories.
With a heart that is caring.
A heart with warmness.
A body that has softness around the bones.

The sensation is a mood that presents well-being.
As vanilla can produce a seductive scent.
I bring out the sexiness and addition as a smell of perfume.
There is something about the playfulness of the sweet aroma.
That draws men to their hive.

My skin is described as light.
My skin is described as medium.
My skin is described as olive.
My skin is described as slightly tan.
My characteristics are cozy and clean.

I dress in neutral tones such as white.
Such as beige.
Such as light brown.
Such as light blue.
I favor knit sweaters.
I love leggies.
I love my Uggs footwear.

My scent is like the taste of marshmallows.
I am a beautiful match for all races.
My voice attracts all the men in my radius.
I will not allow anyone to take my innocence.
As the world symbolizes me with purity.

Wedding Cheer

A toast to the bride and groom.
Together you shall stand.
The both of you are a united family.
Your offspring will become a blessing.
May you get through the rough and tough times.

There will be good and bad times.
There will sickness and health.
When we took each other hands.
From this day forward for better or worse.

If we become rich or poor.
Our business stays in our home.
Only we can make our situation improve.
We shall be each other strength.
We shall work to overcome each other weaknesses.

Through both of our faults.
As we offer ourselves.
I choose you to be my wife.
I chose you to be my husband.
Until we part ways by death.

Through all our us and downs.
We shall become best friends.
We shall be each other biggest fan.
We shall root for each other.
As we shall solemnly swear.

What A Man Sees in a Woman

I see my woman what other men do not see.
I see a part of my mother and grandmother in her.
Not all the qualities but the ones that remind me of them.
Do I want her to be the same as them.
The answer is no but it is the opening that flows through a man's heart.

She can be a city woman or a country woman.
She can be from a different country.
A man may have date many women to find the right one.
Not just as he is lusting but looking to gain a soulmate.
A future they can build upon.

Maybe she is quite or maybe she is loud.
Maybe she is adventurous or maybe she is a homebody.
A man knows what he wants in a woman.
If he sees what he wants he will come after her.
He looks for the major qualities which is a short list.

The choices are different in all men.
From the perfume he smells to the sound of her voice.
If he is connected to her like a magnet.
She will be his gracious prize.
From the whites of her eyes to the shape of her thighs.

A man sees if a woman can be his wife.
A man sees if a woman can be a great mother to his kids.
A man sees if a woman can be independent.
A man sees if a woman would stand by him.
A man sees if a woman would be faithful.
A man sees id a woman would be loyal.

A man goes by what he sees.
All men do not find what they are searching for.
A man wants a woman around his arm.
Every man needs a woman to evolve.
A man looking for success needs that woman by his side.

What I Look For In A Woman

A man looks for in a woman to stand by him.
A man looks for in a woman to be in his corner.
A man looks for in a woman to lift him up.
A man looks for in a woman to support him.
A man looks for in a woman to emotion stability.

A man looks for in a woman to be grounded.
A man looks for in a woman to keep him motivated.
A man looks for in a woman with a sense of humor.
A man looks for in a woman is ambition.
A man looks for in a woman kindness.

A man looks for in a woman is independence.
A man looks for in a woman is building a family.
A man looks for in a woman is respect.
A man looks for in a woman is commitment.
A man looks for in a woman decisiveness,

A man looks for in a woman is dependability.
A man looks for a woman to be honest.
A man looks for a woman to be intelligent.
A man looks for in a woman to be understanding.
A man looks for in a woman to be kind-hearted.

A man looks for in a woman is reliability.
A man looks for in a woman to be courteous.
A man looks for in a woman is integrity.
A man looks for in a woman are values.
A man looks for in a woman to have morals.

A man looks for in a woman being a communicator.
A man looks for in a woman to be an excellent mother.
A man looks for in a woman is to be appreciated.

A man looks for in a woman is to be loved.
A man looks for in a woman to be his wife.
A man looks for in a woman is to grow old with her.

What Is A Good Woman

I want to take this time to give respect that is due.
To the woman of my world that made a difference or two.
She is smart like a scholar. Voice that can be heard.
Who is aware of who she is.

She inspires her man to be the best.
Do not have to stand in front as she is the rock behind his success.
She gives her kids the confidence to strive above others.
She is a daughter, sister, aunt, wife, and mother.

She is the glue that holds the family together.
She is fearless.
She is a role model and worth more than gold.
Mental strength that men can't hold.

Sensitive to the needs as she takes plight.
Mentors to young girls to cross woman hood.
Many characteristics makes up a good woman.
She is proud of what she brings.

Many women can assume this title.
Many women can't live to the standard.
It takes a real woman to hold the torch to the light.
There is no substitute for a good woman.

A person who is well spoken.
A person who comes in the clutch.
A person who never stop believing in her husband.
A virtuous woman who always prays.

She knows the difference from selfness and selfish.
The power of forgiveness.
Woman is the title of a female.
A title that is earned not a title to call.

Who is she?
Where is she at?
Can you see her?
Bold and confident.

She has the blessings that is the behold.
For the love of a good woman.
The righteous of encouragement.
There is no other to take her place.

Why I am Light-Skinned

I am light skinned because of two races.
Different in color and different in background.
Two people of different backgrounds.
Came together because of love.

Which race should I accept.
Who should determine which race I belong to.
Why I can't be acceptable to both.
As I am mixed with both sides' bloodline.

I belong to two of the challenging races.
That struggle to find their places.
As history has taught us that one race was not kind to another.
Thus, we still face challenges to this day.

One race does not accept me.
The other one gives me a hard time.
My parents are my rock.
I must brave the fight on my own.

One race says I am not light enough.
The other race says I am not dark enough.
Where do we as a people draw the line?
Why can't we accept each other as people?

I am light skin.
Proud to be light skin.
I should have the best of both worlds.
I am the link to both races.
I will die light-skin.

You Are The Reason

You are the reason that I am crazy about you.
You are the reason that I am attractive to you.
You are the reason that I stay focused.
You are the reason I stay in line.
You are the reason of me that I can strive above obstacles.
You are the reason I can work with confidence.
You are the reason I can be myself.
You are the reason this family is together.
You are the reason that our household is together.
You are the reason I can walk with my head high.
You are the reason I do not want to leave.
You are the reason I smile.
You are the reason I can laugh.
You are the reason I can joke.
You are the reason I can walk a path.
You are the reason I have goals to attain.
You are the reason I have a home to come to.
You are the reason I am in love with you.

You are the reason for everything.

www.ingramcontent.com/pod-product-compliance
Lightning Source LLC
Chambersburg PA
CBHW032212040426
42449CB00005B/554